A Treasury of Trees

For
Anne-Marie

A Treasury of Trees

David Donaldson

Wynstones
Press

Published by
Wynstones Press
Stourbridge
England.

www.wynstonespress.com

First edition 2017

Printed in UK.

ISBN 9780 946206 810

Contents

View from the Ramparts

Epilogue

Prologue

That Seed

The seed and root of all planted
In earth, air, water, light and warmth,

Has known the continents to shift,
Glaciers to advance, retreat,

Outgrown the searching reach
Of dinosaurs and bedded down

In coal and peat. And whether
In arid or in foggy wastes,

In humid heat or cold extremes
Or any climate in between,

It's made a home, it's put down roots
And hoisted shoots. And grown.

Mangrove

... and let dry land appear ...

Sea thunders ashore to swallow up what's going on
Beyond the sanction of its salty sufficiency. But the Lord's
Heard Land's appeal. The Resistance has been launched

On wave after wave of collapsing surf; propagules root –
Ready for action. On landing, they root in mud
And growing, stand clear like stilts to brace their trunk

And house their leaves. Special forces move in to filter out
The choking salt, while trunk and leaves inhale oxygen
To relieve the anoxic condition of the mud. All along

The coasts, the Resistance grows. Sea's advance
Sinks back sucking, swirling round and round but finds
No grip while the growing network sifts its continual wash,

Reclaims sediment. Against Sea's swallowing odds,
Land extends. All surge and fury is disarmed, filtered
Through a dense forest maze of roots which calm

And quieten. Fish arrive to spawn; oysters, barnacles,
Sponges congregate. So also wading birds, raptors,
Reptiles, mammals large and small. Land grows free

Of Sea's cold mothering. Starts out on a life of its own.

The Trees

Our roots entwined with theirs, our language
Still fumbling to translate their speech;
Earth's most far-reaching Word, sounded
In its arboreal force of life erupting
To colonise the land as glaciers retreat.

Oak, ash, alder, birch... wherever we look
Near and far their advance, and others
Massed and massing in their millions
Over plain and hill, undulating waves
Of pathless green, the lofty canopy

Admitting dappled light to the bushy
Undergrowth and its wild sustenance.
Rustle of foraging creatures, sudden
Crash and flight of startled deer towards
A distant glint: spring-fed pool or marsh.

And here, on the forest floor, where feet
Sink into soft depths of rotted leaves,
We pause, clear a space for ourselves,
A home on the pillared threshold
Of the forest boundless in its mystery:

Its dark perils, its hospitality to our needs.

The Green Dream

Hentland

*A parish within the Archenfield Group
of parishes, Herefordshire*

All legend now. And resonance of old names grown apart,
As 'The Land of the Hedgehogs' lies curled up in the name

Of Archenfield. So, as growth rings within ever-widening
Circles the vanished settlement south of the Old Church

Itself the Gospel taken root here centuries before
The ministries of Rome. Long past also, Dubricius,

Hentland's patron saint, his pregnant mother thrown
Into the Wye only to survive and still deliver the child
Destined to heal the leper-king her dishonoured father.

And long buried the favoured erchin at Dubricius' feet,
And his monastery of the Brethren nearby.

Stories like leaves bedded down: rich nourishment
To connect with what remains: the lipwell, still flowing,

Threading its way through shade beside this later church
And subsiding graves, part a managed wilderness. Is it
Favoured of hedgehogs? And beyond the churchyard wall,

Meadow grasses where the settlement once stood
And the air whispering in ancient trees.

Beech Wood

As you drive, it appears abruptly: an entering-in to wonder at,
The light dappled green in spring, sudden welcome shade
In summer; in autumn an avenue of gold and fire overarching

The road. It was gifted to the village over a century ago,
The tumbled boundary walls once served with signs offering
Rewards for information... though they've never been repaired.

Up, early one summer morning, notebook in hand. Nothing
Stirring save for the scuffling of a mouse. But all those
Obscure tracks through undergrowth to understorey hideaways...

The lanky beeches were cathedral-high and we, as in the hushed
Interior of an empty stately house were free to rush about, climb,
Explore. We'd slither down the sheer sides of quarried hollows

To rummage among the treasures of The Dump: old pram wheels
For trolleys? Tearing along leaf-mould corridors belly-flat,
Juddering over roots, we'd steer to the Niagara of bare steep slopes,

The final swoop and plunge of the trolley-run. Now the dump's
No more, the slope has seeming-shrunk. But the trees are still
Cathedral-high, an avenue to amaze and at my feet today,

Things I gave no heed to as a child: seedlings scattered all about
In the wood's dark mould. A few to lift, carry home and plant
For a garden hedge, a sheltering perimeter; like this beech wood

Itself, a stately home within which we put down roots and grew.

Hazel

Shade within shade.

Humble understorey tree
Supreme in wisdom. One

Of the three most precious
Unbreathing things. Each

Leaf a green pool drawn
From the well of earth;

Its rain of catkins a fine veil
Parting winter from spring.

Dappled shade in summer
As nutshells harden, small

Cauldrons of inspiration

Once votive offerings
Cast into pools and wells.

Hazelnuts. Old-fashioned
Wealth. Sources of health,

Embracing us from skin
To bones; from our digestion,
Nerves, muscles, joints,

To our blood and beating hearts.

Old Hazel Tree

A patch of hillside slipped away and there
Holding the bare earth in place, a solitary
Hazel tree; free to stretch and spread, be
Unconfined under the one shared sky.

The squat trunk's a dozen stems welded
Into one, griffin paws delving to grip
The sloping ground. It's a green world
All its own. A jostling of generations,

Its low shelter continuing down the hill
And yards to either side, the earth strewn
With the gnawed remains of nuts. Shoots
From the knuckled trunk have provided

Tender grazing while others, perpendicular
On the lower branches have shot up
Out of reach, adding youthful growth
To ageing thicknesses. And, as if

To double their support, older branches,
Crossing over have bedded each into
The other. A green inclusive world
This world of Hazel and its hazelnuts!

Oak Tree

A royal summit, crowned and waving.
A watchtower over miles and years.
Pillar trunk raising a cathedral space,
Roof-dome in constant motion
Its own mystery long since served

By its buried acorn and the summons
Of sun, wind, rain to this one patch
Of earth. The strength here to sail
The seas, hold up a hundred roofs,
Scatter its largesse of acorns from

Bunched twig tips, its greenwood face
Of leaves lobbed and leathery; and heal
Its scars and wounds from the dead
Or sawn-off remnants of old campaigns,
Once the blazing fuel of winter hearths.

Sweet Chestnut

Canopy of cavernous shade. Lowest boughs
Spread to the measure of the trunk's girth,
The spiral swirl of the furrowed bark its staircase

Over centuries to heights which now look down
From tier on clustered tier of long serrated leaves,
Cliff overhangs each the launch site for rays

Of flowering stalks. From base to tip each bears
The forming prickly balls set to tumble in the Fall
And even now teetering on the sloping brink

Of the leaf edge. Tree of Olympian Zeus;
Of astringent leaf, of bark and wood. Granary
Of staple nourishment; battle food of the Legions.

The rustling of its leaves is like a rhythmic
Sharpening of blades to renew its cutting edge.

Consider the Trees

Young trees reach branches skywards,
Form a receiving chalice for the sun's
Light and warmth. Up, up they reach

As year on year their growth displays
What they've received. You might think
Their only wish were to tower to heaven

And on and up forever and ever.

Older trees know otherwise: their glory
And their measure is to receive
A crown: their ever-thirsting chalice

Turned upside-down. Its rim no longer
Taking in but describing the circle
Of a full-grown fruitful Presence.

Hornbeam

A tiered hillside you may stoop and enter,
Roots like dark knuckles, twisted flows of iron,
The trunk an effort of diminishing girths:

Father, mother, child, welded together
And rusty-red where the bark's peeled off.
The lower boughs are only shoulder high

As if no time's been spared in pushing out
Each gravity-defying yard. They bristle
With black wheals of witches' broom,

Charcoal smudges as though smouldering
From the inside. But looking up is to lose
Yourself in an aerial forest: trunk,

Boughs, branches merge in a green density
Concealing summit, sun and sky so that
Your defeated gaze returns to cool

Tranquillity, the shaded reach
At your feet. Earth in repose
Within a dome of fresh green leaves.

Alder

The Monnow at Skenfrith

A riverside colony. Aged pioneers on top of the bank,
Root-base out of sight, except for limbs tumbling
To anchor in the water's rapid course and follow on

Downstream, the younger generation born not of seed
But root and hoisted as if on rafts in the river's shallows.
Elsewhere, root-works exposed by the water's wash,

Have engineered an island-mound of pipes and knobs
A dozen trunks stacked on top. Lowest branches extend
Over the water, storm-litter caught on twigs, catkins

Brushing the surface; and one bough, plunged into the bank,
Has tunnelled back to the top, emerged full-branched,
As though a Tree in its own right swaying with catkins,

Its empty cones left overwintering, signalling of futures
Long since flown – yet always present, like water's flow,
Its rise and fall, in constant cycles of return.

The Green Dream

'Sans Souci', Val d'Illiez

Clock ticks soften the silence of the rafters,
The wood panelling, the granite stove.
But open the door and the forest's roaring,
The giant's grey face, rocky-sheer above
Its bristling beard of mountain pine one
Sleeping frown. Tumbled into place
On the forest floor, great boulders rest,
Loosed singly or in volleys, relics

Of a past long since withdrawn into itself
And greened-over by moss-settlers: feathery
Carpet-cushions moist and bright moulding
Jagged edges out of sight or hanging,
Curtain-wise, over cracks and crevices
Where roots have set to work to stake
Their claim to home. Stems stretch high,
Branches lift pinnate leaves like flags

To celebrate a victory that everyone
Can share: dark green spires of pine,
Fern-fountains gushing out of deep gashes,
Fungal spores powdering scarred rocky faces,
Lichens stamping their tatoos. This wide-
Strewn titanic wreckage has turned into
Hives of green activity, its damp silence
Drowned out by water's roar. Edge closer

To a curtained residence, peer in:
Unblinking eyes stare back at you from
A dark recess. So far and no further. Would
You shatter the green dream? You return,
Close your door and the river's roar fades.
You're back with the clock's tick; with
The silence of the rafters, the panelled wood
All hewn from this forest: from the green dream

Where those unblinking eyes met yours.

Young Pine

When I bought you, trussed up in a net,
You were about waist-high. Now you're
Twice my height, curved extending branches

A redoubt of pricking needles of such a length
It's small wonder your kind fell out of favour
As Christmas trees. How they'd fend off

Eager fingers reaching to place those
Tinsel baubles! On our slope you stand aloof
Among Hazel, Birch as the autumn breezes

Swirl their leaves adrift. You let nothing go.
Ever-green, solemn, candle-tips deep down
Within their needle chalices ghostly white.

You're one majestic candelabra that will never
Quite catch fire, open blossoms to the sun.
Too absorbed in your own mystery for that.

Conifer Wood

That stillness on entering. Solemn.
Slow. As if someone's hardly
Breathing. Only the topmost quarter
Is needle-green. The rest's already
Battle-dead, stiff and snapped,

Some branches dangling twigs
Frail as cobwebs or threadbare
Like decomposing flags.
Their greenery's composting
At your feet, compounding

The silence of your tread. Here
And there holes for investigation
Have been scuffed from the bare earth,
Creatures now curled underground
In the daytime darkness of their setts.

continued over...

Looking up, you'd hardly know
It was a cloudless October day.
All feels withdrawn, a world
To itself, a present arrested
Long ago even though these trees

Towering ram-rod straight
Are young and ready-made for use.
They wind back the ages to a time
Before trees knew how to leaf, flower,
Conceive a crown. Their needles

Bristling, their woody cones,
Their bark weeping with the outflow
Of their flammable flower-force
Held back. Forever smouldering
        In resin.

Broadleaf Wood

That stillness. But nothing here's
Withdrawn into silence, unable
To be uttered. A green arcade
Of Hazel. Dappled shade

Of quiet peace. The round
Leaves like big water-drops.
A sense of sunlit fruitfulness,
No muffled tread shuffling

Through the faint rasp
Of fallen leaves. And rising
High above, a canopy
Of Chestnut, Oak, foliage

Of Ash fanning out against
The blue, letting it sail through,
Earth-rooted in its towering
Contemplation of the heights.

Ash

Legendary sustainer of the three Worlds.
You leave us standing earthbound, small.
Straining our necks to follow you up and up.

Even where your trunk divides, your boughs
Still climb sheer. Branches may bow
To gravity, decline as steeply, trailing

Loose leaf clusters close to the ground.
But the lowest twigs will still curl skywards,
Buds black as night as if dreaming-bent

On the golden heights. Sun and air!
What signal joy in your pinnate leaves,
Spread to fan the face of the sun, receive

Your return of full-green nourishment; sway
Like a tall ship at anchor on a gusty sea.
And what joins the heights to the depths

Is your bark, cross-hatched, as of a studied
Rippling up and down of the water your roots
Have drawn from deep underground.

Annunciation

The air makes music out of this surrender:
The evening light a muted grey, the fields
So many contrasted browns; curled leaves
(Worm-food, earth-food) scattered
Or drifted into corners, and the pond

Motionless: a held note all its own, at once
Clear to its murky sediment and darkly
Reflecting. No tragic sunderings. No rage.
The evening's one long-held diminuendo in
An utter absence of desire; a hush of wings

Spread to encircling horizons, a settling
Calm drawing inwards to a zero point
From which the new year will take fire.
It's Mary's moment. When the angel speaks
Her reply is the music of the wintering trees.

Dates and the date Palm

They were always a treat at Christmas,
Close-packed in their narrow wooden box
Glossy-coated and sticky with a long
Bendy prong to lever them out. They too
Were part of the story with the three
Wise Men and the camels silhouetted against
A wintry sky. A welcoming prospect of rest
And refreshment on the arduous journey.

And they were to appear again towards
The end of the story though this time as if
Its promised destination: palm branches
Waving and strewed over the ground
By a crowd eager to be led to the sun-ripe
Oasis of their imagined future. It invoked
War's winning ways, ended with mass
Suicides faced by the Legions at Masada.

How easy to berate such fervour's faulty logic.
But the evasive action of the three Wise Men,
Forewarned in dream, served to scatter
The focus of Herod's wrath over every
Infant male in Bethlehem. And framed
Between these two massacres? A willed
Solitary death. And a detail of like seeming
Insignificance: the seed of a stored date palm,

Recovered after two thousand years among
The rubble and skeletons of Masada –
And planted. As if not to be outdone by
The Christ seed, it returned to life, burst back
Into time, our time, flowered and now stands
Over ten feet tall, its fertilising pollen well set
To produce yet more close-packed, sweet
And glossy-coated nutritious Christmas treats.

Christmas Tree

Enter the tree, to share our hearth,
The green world brought in from the cold
And dark, the frost, the midnight stars,

To be festooned with tinsel-garlands,
Hung with fairy lights and shining globes,
With painted birds and golden coins;

Enter the tree, to act its festive part
Of primal innocence, emblem
Of our nativity all the way from

The topmost angel or crowning star
Down winding tinsel paths to those
Mysterious bright-wrapped parcels

Waiting for us on the floor beneath,
The gifts we're destined to receive, grace
Of the ever-fruitful Christmas tree.

Holly

And the first tree in the greenwood
It was the Holly

Pyramid of evergreen. Spindly
Branches stepped sloping apex
To base. Leaves spick and span
Throughout the waning year
And twisted with warrior-vigour
Into sharp defensive thorns.
Within, storm-shelter for birds,
Dry leaf-litter for creatures
Over-wintering. Darkest of leaves
    Yet the whitest of woods.

Warms with a bright steady flame,
    The heraldic tree of Truth;

Brightens our festivities, white-
Scented May come to its fullness
In the merry berries of December
(The Green Knight in the shadows,
Holly club and axe in hand).

    Then heigh-ho the Holly!

    In deepest darkness
    Those bright berries,
The jewels in Holly's crown.

Weeping Willow

Her crown's loose-fitting. Long tresses
Trail to brush your face or the watery surface
At the river's edge. Is she weeping? If so,
It's not from regret or bitterness. Brought low

With age or storm, she'll put out roots
To grip the earth again, leave her last
Remains hollowing out, food for the living,
Shelter for the earthbound dead. So watery-

Pliable, wands of her willow-kin weave
Cradles, coffins, hurdles, bindings for brooms,
Baskets of every shape. There's witchcraft
In her bark, relief for pain, for freeing

The congested heart. And yet a willow wreath's
For rejected love. Is she weeping our
Unwillingness to heal, forgive?
Those trailing tresses her living fountain.

Magic of moon radiance.

Hawthorn Tree

Whitethorn, hagthorn, ladies' meat or bread and cheese,
Those compact leaves criss-crossed with thorns;
Faery tree of pixie pears and cuckoo beads, whither

Do you lead? Joseph's planted staff on Wearyall,
Christmas blossoms for the Queen or where the great
And good now lie nearby in Westminster, the sacred site

Of Thorney Isle? Or your rag trees for petitions still
Growing beside our healing wells or the may
For newly-weds, their tree of hope (and admonition,

Those blossoms, fading to smell of rotting flesh)?
Oh tree of Hymen, tree of Flora, may queens, maypoles
On the green, while spring's white-fire-narcotic

Plays its part upon the breeze. Spellbound lies
The Flower Bride, Summer stretched on its bed of thorns.
Who will penetrate this guarded thicket, wake to life

Its fruitfulness, warm its ripening blood-red treasure
  For the healing of our hardened hearts? Who
  But the thorn-crowned Lord of the Elements?

Elder Tree

Old Crone. Heavy-wrinkled.
Spongy to the touch. Wasted arms
Spotty with warts, thin wands
Reaching up, pinnate leaves
Teetering on top casting spells
On the breeze. So ragged

And ungainly, a law
Unto yourself, Old Crone,
Setting up home anywhere
You choose. Your gangling
Lack of charm, your unruly force
Inviting the disrespect towards

Invasive weeds. So you're
Cut down below the knees,
Only to spring back to lead
The summer in with heady
Umbels, cream-white plates
Of flowers: offerings

With which to toast the bride.
You're there again at winter's
Threshold, summer's champagne
Turned to nourishment
Berry-black against the dark
And cold. *Old Girl*, most

Maligned of trees. Knapped
Flints of Elder leaves placed
In prehistoric tombs. Perhaps
We understood you better then,
Your connecting radiance:
Gnarled on the outside, inside

Dissolving-soft; your powers
To transform, regenerate.
There you are in the hedge,
Peering out between Hazel,
Leylandi. I ask your blessing.
Stay by our back door.

Rowan

The Quicken Tree. All light, air and activity,
Pinnate leaves raised fan-wise to the sun.
The slender trunk's a gracious outcome of

Tenacious roots in unaccommodating soils.
Here's a white blossom fresh as May
(Though it's September) and berry-clusters,

Some still infant-green, while others long
Advanced to scarlet have already wrinkled
And now hang black-shrivelled as though

Winter were already here. Tree of charms.
A Portal Tree where life, death, rebirth
Manifest in one. And nowhere knuckled

Gestures of defiance or heavy-armouring.
But the hardy strength of living grace, its bark
Smooth-flecked and shining silver-grey.

Inspiration for the weary, uplift
For the failing or the weak. And everywhere
You look at twig-tips, leaf axils, next year's

Buds nestling like so many hungry beaks.

Silver Birch

An explosive lift-off
For a graceful presence.

Trunk pristine white and smooth
However green-smudged with lichen,
Yet ruptured at base to smatterings
Like snow on upthrust ridges.

Enter *The Lady of the Woods* trailing
Showers of long-extending twigs
To brush the ground. Her cleansing

Besom. Her once-unsparing rods
For schoolboy miscreants; she's
Light, air, fire; *The shining one.*

Brighid's perpetual flame renewing
And renewed. Leaves heart-shaped
Though with serrated edges at once

Pure pointed virgin strength and
Fertile mother; hers the favoured
Maypole wood. Shimmering gold

In autumn. Stripped in winter except
For what still hangs of the year's
Fruitfulness and first to be reclothed

In green. Tireless pioneer transforming
Wasted sites, cindered clearings,
Will root even on scree. For many,

The honoured tree of Pentecost.

Cherry

Part adolescent? Plenty of spring
But a stiffness in the branches
Right into the twigs: something

Withheld, at odds with the story
The buds will crowd to whisper
Out-loud when the time is ripe:

That pale heaven of fragile
Tenderness. Families in Japan
Will gather for the Feast

Of the Sight of the Cherry Blossoms,
Picnics spread in the brief days
Before the breeze disperses heaven

In showers of petals. And well
And good: for what's to follow
Is so more deep-seductive, red

And sweet, inviting you to dip
Time and again into the bowl
Which never empties, as what

You place there in exchange,
Contains the deepest mystery of all:
The stone.

Growing on

I

Ancient Holly Grove

Perpendicular towers balancing branches
High above, stiffened bark overlapping
Like plates of armour, trunks split wide,

Worm holes drilled into dried-out channels,
The young clustering about the roots,
Stretching tall wands. Ever-green. All ages

Growing on. There's gargoyle noses,
Young purple-stippled bark; and sudden
Elbow angles as if a wrestling challenge

Long delivered, were still waiting
To be undergone. So much wrestling!
To heal as well as grow, marked in rings

Like pebble-ripples, spread from lost
Branches or the countless burrs and bulges
That have swelled to seal off scars and wounds.

And there's the middle-aged: no longer green
And smooth but creasing, lightly cracked
Though not yet shrunk and lifting, stiffened hard.

Here's no humble hedge or understorey bush
But Holly in its own right. Growing on against
The grain of gravity: wrestling upwards.

Plunged in earth yet seeking out the sky.

II

Holy Well

Following the hills' level skyline along lanes
Threading steep valley sides, past farms
And ruined cottages and over racing streams,

You'll come to a square metal gate and a field
Sloping steeply to the valley floor. There you'll find
A fenced enclosure to keep out trampling animals.

For a spring emerges here among an ancient
Holly grove, the bole of an Ash squat on top
Of the opening in the hillside. Here movement

And stillness merge as one. A pool never emptying,
Making its way over stones and spreading into moss.

Water as ever-present and unmarked by cycles
Of growth and decay, as the weathered Hollies bear
Evergreen forces of renewal to their slender wands.

Pure water spilling out of the all-giving Earth.
The ancient Hollies self-healing, growing on.

Old Oak

On guard in all directions: massive paws
Of statuary creatures; or the lava-spills
Of its once molten growth, inscribed
In endless runic patterns now smoothed
As if to weathered stone. So heavily
Defended, this fortress oak! Even so

It's been overrun, wind and weather
Its life-support and besieging enemy.
The lower trunk's now hollowed out,
The impregnable tower of its leading shoot
Collapsed; framed spaces left gaping
Where boughs once radiated. And yet,

Witness its will to heal, sail on still
Living-bouyant, in the rings of bark
Clustering to seal off lost limbs. One
Remains, jutting out, a ghost ship's
Splintered figurehead. And on the trunk's
Reverse, two chinks in the armour peer out,

Like watchful eyes weathering to stone.

Yew

Wintergreenest tree works on
In low light and winter's
Dormant cold, neither
Conifer nor broadleaf,

Simply Yew – slow but sure,
In time outpacing everyone.
Churchyard guardian
Of mysteries, the Tree

Of trees? Its 'apple'
The rightful fruit of Eden?
Tempting-sweet about
A deadly kernal, a cure

For cancer in the poison
Of its leaves. And far
Horizons in the silent
Pulse of its longevity.

View from the Ramparts

Olive

Athene's founding gift.
Cradle-tree of the west.
Trusted temple-scaffolding
To the Greeks and their gold-green heart,

The pressed oil their vision
Of harmony and health,
Spring's blossom-fragrance
Uniting with the harvest's astringent fruit.

Year on year, to them
This yield of light,
Nourishment, cleansing.
Oil for anointing athlete and priest.

War in abeyance.
Peace and victory in embrace.

The more gnarled the ageing trunk
The more the forces it's wrestled

From the earth. Now old dwellings
Stand derelict, their terraces a tangle

Of neglect. But the ancient olives
Are still fruiting as though all were

As it used to be, the animals browsing
Or resting under their shade,

The young still at home, chafing
    At their inheritance.

           *

Cradle-tree of the west. And still rocking us!

Abandoned trees may disappear overnight
And reappear transplanted in a holiday lot –

Or sold on for their venerable mystique
To grace, alfresco, a fashionable restaurant,

The silvered leaves, lancet-tipped and evergreen,
Soaking up the sun and here and there,

Their substance offered up, falling out of use
About conversing heads, not as the seasons

    But as Olive's particular needs dictate.

Dawn Redwood

Metasequoia

First, entered into the fossil record
Then, discovered alive and well,
Living in China. From dead

Mineral to elegant fluted trunk,
Soft bark the colour of cinnamon.
A conifer, ancestral line traced

To the warm shallow seas
Of the Cretaceous, dinosaurs
Grazing nearby. A stand-alone,

Stepped into the sun, never one
For the forest gloom, the play
Of its feathery leaves filtering

The light. Suddenly, as if mere
Moments ago in geologic time,
We wake- are woken up- to this

Sunny conifer from the World's
Dawn. Water Fir returned to re-
Populate a transformed Earth,

Gracing our parks and streets.

Lime Tree

Takes its time. For the first half century
Finding its feet, then quickening into its future,
The grey-ridged trunk, fine-fingered mesh
Of branches, low hanging canopy and crown
Of open-hearted leaves stepped out of the forest,
Become a sanctuary where safety might be sought,
Truth divined in its court of law, justice delivered.

A thousand years may pass and its own
Inwoven story change: Frigga's tree of fertility
Become the wood of icon painting, carvings
Of the Christian story. It's responsive
To our pruning, pollarding, from imposing
Civic tree to pleached garden hedge; a hive
Of blossoms in sweet-scented June, choirs of bees

Making the air vibrate into midsummer nights,
And free in the overflow of all it is and has
To give within and beyond our categories of beauty,
Utility, convenience: embracing aphids equally
With bees, the effluent of their 'honeydew' dripping
Without more ado onto whatever's underneath:
Parked cars, smart clothes, our unsuspecting heads.

Ancient Oak

Rule Britannia

King of the waxing year. Still wreathed about
With green leaves when other trees now stand
Windswept and bare. Only its buds' insistent
Push will shake them onto the wintry air.
The trunk's a battlement of bark baked into
Rough crusts of ridges, trenches iron-red
With trails like warm lava flows; it mounts

To a stage from which a dozen limbs thrust
Out or up, framing the leading shoot, a tower
All its own with sprouting room for holly, elder.
Dark stains mark the rains' repeated trickling
To the lower reaches smudged with lichen,
Furry with moss, down to the sphinx paws
That delve deep as the crown's high.

All our story's gathered here: inscribed
In Oak, whether as timber or sheltering
Circumference; as unrecorded Druidic lore
Or the first casting of the Runes; reverent
Wonder; the hush of superstitious fear.
A Chieftain Tree. Guardian Oak attracting
To itself the lightning stroke, beneath which

Tribal kings were crowned, which marked
The heart and moot of countless settlements
Oak-names still imprinted on our maps;
A power space to be fought over, seized
Or razed; under whose shade pigs were fattened,
Couples married, the Gospel preached;
Out of whose wildwood the Green Man stepped

To rule the waves.

Alder

Not so much free-standing trees
As pioneering communities
On mounds of spongy roots,

Arboreal marsh villages root
By root extending a mesh
Of earth beneath their shade.

Leaves rounded but for a dint
As if their tips had dripped like
Waterdrops to join their kind:

Water and earth,
Water and earth.

Wetnurse of the woodlands,
Transferring nursling land
To oak and ash. And how

Supportive, pile-driven into mud,
Waterlogged against decay,
Still holding up our marsh cities.

Venice. Amsterdam.

Coconut

*Kalpaviksha: the tree that provides
everything for life*

Light. Air. Warmth. And the forest
Lightly swaying in the sea-breeze,
The long leaf-fronds riding the air
Seeds scattering or already afloat
Bound for the open ocean or landfall
And a new start. It's easy to feel

Lulled here. Languid in the heat,
The high sun and the forest stretching
Out of sight in airy spaciousness as if
There were no end to its sunlit shade,
The cultivated plots, the animals
Browsing. All needs met. Bullock carts

Rumble by dwellings grown out of
The forest timber, its fibrous leaves,
As also the woven floor coverings,
Household implements, baskets,
Rope, twine, the oiled shine
On your skin. And there's the fruit

Tumbling to your feet as from
The heavens of every tree. You drink,
Eat, use it for cooking. And to Lakshmi,
To three-eyed Shiva you offer thanks
Each day, from the scooped-out
Shell of the three-eyed coconut.

Rubber Tree

Lines stretching up a hill. It's not the sap
We're after. That's deeper in. But the trees'
Surface system of self-defence carried

To sticky, milky-white extremes. Ducts
Of latex guarding the cambium against
All-comers. So extraordinary a chemical

Rebounds in world-wide frenzy to exploit,
Once the processing is understood beyond
Its native use for balls and toys. Seeds

Close-guarded in Brazil suddenly turn up
At Kew. Regimented work forces empire –
Wide marshalled to serve their masters' will.

Tribes, stripped of every native self-defence,
Enslaved to keep production up. Henry Ford
Steps in. Rubber's on the move! Tappers,

At work by dawn with skillful cuts careful
Not to pierce the cambium. Every other
Day or so, tree by tree for years the little

Buckets are suspended to catch
The steady colloidal drips.

Douglas Fir

As telegraph poles
It carries wires
Upright beside
Its sleepers laid
To span the continents
With railways.

Cocoa Tree

Cauliflory, understorey,
Leave the forest as it is
So undisturbed the little
Pollinating insects may
Continue with their work.

No intermediary of leaf
Or twig. Directly each
Green pod will spring
And hang from branch
Or trunk, a rugby ball

Of ripening beans whose
Great good fortune
(Or its fate) is never ever
To lose a game, as once
Touched down it's then

Converted into chocolate.

Mahogany

Dug-out canoes gave them the idea.
They piled their plundered treasures
Into such treasured ships as set
The English off in hot pursuit of both.

Later old hulks turned into prized lots,
Centres of recycling for fine furniture
Built to last, until the trials of fashion
Passed sentence on the antique 'Brown Mile'.

But then, a brief revival during the War.
That heavy fusty furniture taking to sea
Once more. Minesweepers of mahogany
Against the menace of magnetic mines,

Blast-proof, shock-proof as Old Ironsides.

View from the Ramparts

Where we once stood sentinel,
Our homely fires smoking
In the clear air, the hillside ringed
With ramparts from which

We watched for movement
On the silent tangled plain below,
Oak, ash, sweet chestnut
Have moved in to take our place,

The abandoned ramparts now
A tangle of bracken, brambles,
Greying willowherb; an occupying
Stillness, a leafy peace of trees,

Of the thump of chestnuts falling.
While the silent plain's become
One unresting roar as of something
Woken up and hungry. Stand

Sentinel here once more. What's
Moving there below? What
Is it, this roar that seems to say:
'Feed me. Feed me. I need

More and ever more.'

Yew Conscripted

The mountains shorn of their pristine
Monumental stands. Traded in
For a royal slaughter of men; the hum
Of bowstrings, flights of arrows thick enough
To darken the sky at Crecy, Agincourt.

Yew conscripted. Hewn down to serve
Our wars. What if the skill to pluck out
Wood both of heart and sap, fashion it
To deliver death and injury, the power
To pierce armour or a stout oak door,

Had power also to restrain the hasty arrow
Already aiming at the next best thing
For laying waste to empower, enrich?
Could persuade those clenched fingers
To slacken their grip on the straining string?

Gum: Eucalyptus Tree

That appealing native picture:
Kookaburra perched in the old
Gum tree, or possum, koala
Nosing the menthol-fragrance
Of the leaves; but the small
Desert, leaf-littered beneath

Tells another story: of the one
Spark which could set the whole
Neighbourhood ablaze,
Invoke Gum's working ways
With fire, its oils adding fury
To the flames making a clean

Sweep so buds deep-buried
In its trunk or underground,
Will be the first to shoot after
All's laid waste. So the spread
Of Gum's assured. And gathers
Pace beyond its native shores.

For the cry goes up at its invasive
Reach as though a monster
Were on the move, a wildfire
Driving poor folk from their
Tiny plots of corn, their use
Of its wood for life's necessities,

(And resting beneath its welcome shade).
Gum's working ways with fire
Are no less assured when the fire
Takes on human form, makes
Clean sweeps and when that's done,
Plants vast acres of Gum for pulp.

Giant Sequoia

Wellingtonia

Require scorched earth to spread themselves
And thrive, the ground fire-fertilised, the heat
Fierce enough to spring seeds clear from tight –
Fisted cones while leaving themselves untouched
Up there, clad in spongy fire-resistant bark.

Some of an age to be a living link with
The Great Pyramid and taller than Big Ben.
Favoured of rich Victorians, their adopted
Tree Imperial its towering impress a measure
Of the times, the ground clean-razed

From under a rural population sacrificed
To the blaze, expendable human fuel
Consumed in the mass production of goods,
The mills, mines and factories so many
Blackened fire-blasted cones pouring out

Their seeds of manufacture and growing
Trade gargantuan in quantity. Stranded now,
Domesticated in their parklands, mansions,
Former rectories, the ageing giants stand
Powerless to regenerate themselves without

The heat of wildfire making its clean sweep.

Cork Oak

Unmistakeable, its extreme armouring.
Spongy-strong and rugged. A cratered
Landscape hollowed out as of extinct

Volcanoes wryly suggesting 'no fire here'.
And no cunning survival strategies
Either, for its seeds to get ahead. Oak's

Answer to fire is to dress up in cork
And hold its ground, and that's enough.
Enough, too, for us to benefit from

Its many uses, the slopes it's held
In cultivation for centuries, the water
It retains in thirsty months, the thousands

Employed in skilled labour to safely
Harvest the bark. Armoured in cork,
Oak's ringed about with the Law's defence

In Portugal. A grateful response to its
Response to fire: insulation that keeps
The life-warmth in while keeping the fire out.

Neem

and the corporate Brain Tree

In arid heat and drought, still
To survive and thrive; evergreen,
Wide-spreading shade, long
Leaves waving the air through.

Dried and burnt, they repel
Insects or crushed and soaked
Make an insecticide. Welcomed
In temple precincts, along

The street, in your backyard or
At your wedding to ward off evil
And infection. Its tender shoots
And flowers are a food ingredient,

Its olive-like drupes pressed for
Their *Wonder Oil*, medicinal,
Cosmetic, a lubricant for the ox cart.
The Village Pharmacy, its range

And potency confirmed
By corporate scrutiny. Which
Would be as welcome as
Neem's wide-spreading shade,

Were its Brain Tree not so
Peculiar a species, being one
Known to lay its host environments
To waste and be possessive

Of every commons as by
    The right of Might.

The Cedars of Lebanon

and the Epic of Gilgamesh

On the table in front of me, a cedar cone,
A squat barrel, a skep for its winged seeds.
Tree of fragrant resin, and resonance
As once remote from us as now those
Mountain gods in *the Country of the Living*.

*

Its burst of growth slows as the years pass
Into centuries, the centuries into millennia.
Its commanding height and girth
Supports boughs of a wide-spreading disposition
As if thereby defining the horizon:

Open in all directions.

So enter Gilgamesh
Looking to wrestle down terrors and mysteries,
Slay the evil guardian of a lofty pristine wilderness,
Fell its giant trees and so advance his name
And the prosperity of his city on the plain.

Earliest of recorded tales as if our latest,

Needful, driven, tragic.

*

A cedar, now hemmed in with
Overgrowth of streets, shops and flats,
Its boughs lopped in places, a stray
From former parkland built over,
A grand anomaly stranded here

Yet its right to life too well-
Established to be revoked. What
Wealth and status was it planted
To display? So seeming-settled
And as far from ancient Uruk

As from such giant-terrors
Long overcome – or displaced,
Rather, to new wildernesses,
New endeavours, the challenges
No less, nor the dangers. To be

Righteous (says the Psalmist)
Is to be *Tall as the Cedars of Lebanon.*
And their felling yields Isaiah
A metaphor: for the like fate
Awaiting *the lofty and the proud.*

Thoughts in a Redwood Forest

The wide well-trodden paths lined either side
With rails. And we're free to wander, feel
Over-awed and humbled, no trace of fear:

Safe in the presence of giants, their weight
Of silence, the somnambulent peace;
Remnants of a lost unbounded world

Of perpetual mist, shape-shifting uncertainties,
Trials of named and nameless terrors;
Of worlds within worlds before light itself

Had penetrated water's prism, unveiled
The rainbow world we've taken in mind
To bind, dissect, banishing all that fails

To be caught in the microscopic mesh
Of our mental nets; exchanging what's living
For what's dead in new wildernesses wide-

Awake with self-created ills and terrors.

Thoughts of a Conifer Plantation

We've a lot to think about. Being brought closer together
Has focussed our power of thought. It's discouraged
The birds and the sun's light and those tiresome tangles
That can arise at one's feet. Sheer concentration of spent
Thought-needles has put paid to that: it's the best mulch
For peace and quiet... You say we've grown too self-absorbed?
Well, thinking separates you out, means you keep somethings
To yourself. It hardens you, it's true: the wood overwhelms
The flower. But we like it like that. Do you understand?
Keeping the sun in check, dimming it down. All that blazing
Ardour pouring out and everybody springing to attention,
Glorying in their perfumed costumes and giving thanks- it's
Just not us. We can't stand the rambling variety it creates
And as for those outrageous roses... No, we prefer to stand
Apart, think our own thoughts. Keep your tinder dry, that's what
We say. And we've had a dream. Did you know? It's risen
Among us out of our silent depths. It speaks to our inmost
Self: we call it- Resin. It holds the flower-force back. Yes,
We've a lot to think about. We see now that we're different
From the crowd: our sun-juice, that's the difference: we
Can choose what our flower's to be. We think about it day
And night. Imagine: one spark – and we could set the world alight!

Lombardy Poplar

Tidy, perpendicular habit. A stately avenue
Fit for a mansion or windbreak staking out
Your property; or – to keep you company

Along the level road to the vanishing point
On the flat horizon, leaves in tremulous
Motion, now silver-white, now darker hues

Of green; flickering in and out of day and night;
This life and the otherworld of whispering souls
Clustered on the far shore, lost for where to go.

Yew Tree

Much Marcle, Herefordshire

Lamp light and dark flames. Palms
Of green once waved to honour the Saviour.
The trunk's a cave of whorls: hieroglyphs

Long predating the medieval church
It now bears witness to, the earth
Itself pushed up into a wooded hillock

Of shadowy foliage. It's both dead
And alive; at once a dried-out seabed
And a rising tide of shoots, upright

As the year's new growth and old
As the tonnage of its lower limbs
Weighed onto a frame of iron supports.

Sit in its weathered porch and time
Goes into reverse. Kings and queens
Reel by; Doomsday is unwritten,

The Conquest not yet planned nor yet
The Viking terror setting the coasts alight.
Finally its root takes hold. And as the land

Delivers up this sapling yew another
Seed is being sown: Augustine's mission
To the Angles from Christian Rome.

A's for Apple

From the mountains of Kazaksthan,
Each five-star fruit its own
Forest of diversity, never
Fruiting like its parent tree.

Sweet? Sour? Inedible?
And all the flavours in between.
There's magic in the Apple lottery.
Tourists may peek
Into your backyard
To glimpse the Tree
Of World renown
You planted with that
Random pip from your apple pie.

And Merlin may be sleeping now
But awake, he taught
Beneath the Apple boughs.

And still they come:
From Butterbox to Iron Pin,
From Upton Pyne to Zabergau Reinette,
Those cultivars whose names wear out

A thousand of our alphabets.

'And all was for an Apple...'

Why's the Apple the guilty fruit?
Genesis never mentions it.
Yet it's clear as the picture glass

Capturing Eve reaching
For something too delicious to resist—
A Roman cultivar no doubt,

Or else it might have proved
Too bitter and she'd have had
To spit it out. Perhaps we thought

To point the blame just as
Our salvation was proclaimed
And Apple's mystery had begun

To dawn on us? That willful
Magic, each seed going its own way
And we helpless to change them

(Or our own crabbed selves),
Without devotion to the patient craft
    Of learning how to graft.

Apple Tree

All you hear is the mythology.
The ubiquitous Apple with
The half-moon bite, the sweet
Forbidden taste of knowledge,
Sex and death trailing in its wake;

The golden Apple for the fairest
That lit the Trojan Wars or faery
Apple-magic set on luring you
Into the Otherworld. Yet not
Every apple has been destined

To deceive. Brendan's sails
Were swelled with trusted tales
Of blessed Apples Isles
And Arthur looked for healing
In such a place. If the Fall's

Our journey beyond instinct
To freely taste and choose
Between what's wholesome
And what's not, the Apple's
Wholly innocent and when

Regrafted on the Tree of Life,
Free of the serpent's guilt
And cool, its apple branch
Will stretch to bridge the gulf
Between this World and that

Orchard-Eden we were set
    To tend and dress.

Epilogue

Yew

'To touch – or be touched – by eternity.'
Only the Nine Sisters know
The beginnings of Yew. They

Are the mothering roots,
Perhaps the Muses too.
The trunk is its light-bridge lit

By the flow of the serpent sap,
Sloughed over centuries,
A hermit's oratory or hollow

For the next generation
To move into, take root,
Round out a new trunk

For a new Age. Or boughs,
Once wings widespread
May, in coming to rest,

Take root also, thrust up
Bright new hubs. So Yew
Rounds out our years,

The centuries, Time itself,
Into a grove, a perpetual
Flame of sanctuary.

Trees on the Skyline

New Year's Day 2011

Grey stillness of a winter's afternoon.
The gentle curve of the hill mounts
To trees on the skyline. One glance
And something stirs in me, opens
Up in joy, in love....... of what?

Their crowning presence? Earth's
Royal being in its fullness?
An answering self in me whose
Cycles of becoming, like theirs,
Span centuries, and more – whole

Ages yet to come?

By the same author published by Wynstones Press:
Poems for Younger Children
Promises – A book of Poems

Wynstones Press

publishes and distributes a range of
Books, Advent Calendars, Cards and Prints.
For further information please see:

www.wynstonespress.com
info@wynstonespress.com